THE
COVENTRY
WE HAVE LOST
VOLUME 2

by
David Fry & Albert Smith

SIMANDA PRESS
BERKSWELL 1993

CONTENTS

The compilers would welcome comments and further information. These may be addressed to:

Simanda Press,
Berkswell,
1 Meriden Road,
Berkswell,
Coventry CV7 7BE.

Printed by Warwick Printing Co., Ltd., Theatre Street, Warwick.

INTRODUCTION

We never imagined that our first book would receive such a favourable reaction, making us realise that changes in the suburbs are mourned as much as changes in the City Centre. This second compilation continues the theme of the first, trying to show how many aspects of the City's visual character have been lost this century, but this time concentrating more on the suburbs. The section on the City Centre tends to look more at people and events, but not ignoring the setting.

How much more sensitive to criticism have those who make planning decisions been since the last book? To judge from recent decisions, not at all. The frustrations of many Coventry people at recent developments in the City Centre seem to be due to a lack of an overall plan and a lack of understanding between planners and developers. Although Donald Gibson's original plan for the City Centre was not perfect, he at least worked to an overall concept, a policy which our planners are belatedly adopting. One part of Gibson's plan was the importance of keeping an open vista from the Precinct across Broadgate to the spire of the old Cathedral. Sadly, the view has now been obscured not only by the Cathedral Lanes and its canopy, but also by the intrusive escalator and other developments in the Upper Precinct. The suburbs too have also suffered; a recent example being the felling of 300 year old oak trees in Tile Hill Lane to satisfy the needs of yet another superstore. (What are they doing to the commercial future of the City Centre?) With closer co-operation the road into the site could have been altered to save the trees, if not the hedgerows. Such features are not instantly replaceable; they are an important part of the environment and appreciated by locals as being part of their community. It seems, though, that unless communities campaign in advance of change, important parts of our environment will continue to disappear. Fortunately, some parts of the City have already been designated conservation areas. There are other areas, though, deserving of similar treatment where a careful assessment would reveal many important features that remain unprotected. They need to be safeguarded for future generations.

We have again used contemporary postcards throughout this book to illustrate our theme, and are indebted to the owners of a number of local collections for making them available to us. They are acknowledged inside the back cover. As before we have given an approximate date, based on knowledge of fashions, cars, buildings etc, but in particular, the known period of operation of the postcard publishers and their photographers. Often they were one and the same. Where known their name(s) are given in brackets. Background details of many of these publishers and photographers were given in the first volume.

Broadgate from Hertford Street c1910 (Frederic Lewis)

Smithford Street c1906 (Unknown)

It would be impossible to start any book illustrating Old Coventry without first showing Broadgate, or the 'top of the town' as it was always referred to by Coventry residents. The two postcards chosen on this page somehow typify the memory fixed in the minds of people who remember pre-war Coventry. The first has the cameraman with his back to Hertford Street looking into Broadgate with Smithford Street on the left and High Street to the right. An Edwardian Daimler is at the kerb outside the Kings Head Hotel entrance possibly awaiting a fare to the Railway Station, being pointed in that direction. Directly in front, Cheshire's Windmill Brewery sign is on the 'Royal Vaults' at the entrance into Butcher Row. In the lower picture the other entrance into the Kings Head in Smithford Street can be seen, with an electric tram on its way into Broadgate from either Chaplefields or Earlsdon. The corner of the Kings Head behind the policeman would eventually become Dunn & Co, Hatters.

Hertford Street and Empire Theatre c1916 (A&G Taylor)

This interesting view is looking into Broadgate from Hertford Street, with the post office to the right and Johnson & Mason's premises just beyond on the same side. This building together with the "Coventry Arms" around the corner in High Street, would be demolished in 1929 to enable a new National Provincial Bank to be built when High Street was widened. The Empire Theatre shown to the left was opened in 1907, the foundation stone being laid on 30th June the previous year by Miss Ellen Terry. Later to become a cinema, it remained open even though damaged in the Blitz, until Hertford Street was redeveloped in the 1960's.

Corner of Hertford Street c1931 (Teesee)

Shown soon after it was opened, the new National Provincial Bank on the corner of Hertford Street and High Street, had replaced an earlier Bank of the same name. This together with the 'Coventry Arms' in High Street and Johnson & Mason in Hertford Street had been demolished in 1929 to enable High Street to be widened. The full beauty of this building has now been lost as it can not be viewed in its entirety due to the bridge across Hertford Street.

Hertford Street c1910 (Harvey Barton)

Shown with the Coventry Savings Bank and the post office to the left, in that order, the 'Queens Hotel' was one of the major hotels in Coventry at this period. The entrance to the stable yard at the rear, can be seen to the right of the main entrance. Although the front was badly bombed in the Second World War it remained open, until Hertford Street was redeveloped in 1967.

Kenilworth Castle c1908 (Unknown)

The Kenilworth Castle is typical of many properties in Hertford Street in the early part of the century. This would be a postcard produced for the proprietor, J.T. Woodward, who is proudly standing at the door. The Geisha Cafe can be seen to the right, this being a favourite meeting place for shoppers to have a cream cake and a cup of tea. The Kenilworth Castle closed in 1939, before the War started. The building survived the bombing but was demolished in 1965.

The Tank at Coventry 1918 (Jackson)

In February 1918 to support War Savings Week tank No.119 spent two days in Coventry, and is seen travelling down Hertford Street towards Greyfriars Green where it stayed overnight. This type of tank was made by William Foster Engineers, Lincoln and was fitted with Daimler engines and running gear, made in Coventry. The view shows the Railway Hotel (Peeping Tom) with the entrance into Bull Yard to the left, with the half timbered 'Grapes Inn' on the right, at the entrance into Warwick Lane. This was not the tank that after the War was mounted on a plinth in Greyfriars Green, which was tank No. 143.

Three Tuns Commercial Hotel c1916 (Unknown)

Although this postcard is postmarked 1916, it could well have been produced earlier, as it would be hard to find so many young men not at the War at this time. The occasion would seem to be an outing from the hotel to Kenilworth or Stratford. The entrance into Bull Yard is seen to the right. The Hotel survived the two Wars but not the planners, being demolished in 1965 when Hertford Street and Bull Yard was redeveloped.

Lifeboat Saturday, Smithford Street 1910 (Waterman)

Lifeboat Saturday, The Barracks 1910 (Waterman)

A regular annual event in many towns was the parading of a lifeboat through the streets to raise money for the Royal National Lifeboat Institution, as reliant then as now on voluntary donations. It says something for the romance of the sea that this, the most land-locked of towns, could have so successfully celebrated this event. The second picture shows the means used to display the lifeboat through the streets of Coventry on Saturday 4th June 1910, at the starting point for the procession in the Barracks Square, off Bull Yard. Both the crew and the boat were from Southend-on-Sea having been wined and dined earlier by the Mayor. Various organisations and individuals in fancy dress joined in adding to the carnival atmosphere. As the boat toured the streets of the city centre the crew held out bags on long poles for the crowd to put in their donations. This is shown clearly in the first picture as the boat is hauled up Smithford Street with a couple of trams in the background. The leading crewman looks every inch the salty sea dog!

Barrack's Square 1913 (Unknown)

As well as being the venue for the gathering of people and floats taking part in Pageants and other marches, Barrack's Square was used for many other functions. This picture shows the May Day Horse Parade being judged. It can be seen that soldiers are in the crowd. The billets seen in the background must therefore still be occupied. It would seem that every type of cart and hauliers waggon in use in the city are well represented.

Reform Club c1909 (Harvey Barton)

Although the Reform Club premises still exist in Warwick Row today, without the Ivy and the railings on the front, the building could be quite easily missed. Whilst the cottages next to the Congregational Chapel also exist, they are now shops, the Co-op Bank being next door to the club. On the right hand-side the buildings were demolished in the 1950's, Intershop now being on this site.

Warwick Row c1923 (Photochrome)

This view of Warwick Row is taken from the opposite side of the Congregational Chapel from that of the Reform Club shown on the previous page. The picture is looking towards Hertford Street with all three spires clearly visible. The entrance into Warwick Lane can be seen to the right of Curtis & Beamish, with the entrance into Union Street leading to Christ Church just behind the trees. Just this side of the horse and cart is where Greyfriars Green has now been cut in two by Greyfriars Road.

Queens Road Chapel c1924 (HHT)

The cameraman taking this picture would be standing in Queens Road with the entrance into Queen Victoria Road to the left, where two men can be seen walking. Behind the James Starley Memorial, erected in Queen's Grove in 1884, is the entrance into Warwick Row. The Baptist Chapel does not look quite so grand today as the height of the tower has been greatly reduced. Queens Road is now a dead end as Ringway Queens cuts across just beyond the Chapel.

Rover Ltd c1912 (W.Y.)

Queen Victoria Road c1911 (Harvey Barton)

In the top view, workers are seen leaving the Meteor Works of the Rover Company, walking in Garfield Road, (later to become Rover Road) towards Queen Victoria Road. At this time cars and motorcycles were being built although these works were originally built to produce cycles. The name Rover was originally used for the Safety Bicycle designed by J.K. Starley. A Rover car can be seen parked by the building to the left, but it would appear that very few workers even own bicycles. In the lower picture the Drill Hall can be seen on the immediate left with further down the entrance into Croft Road. Only a small portion of Queen Victoria Road exists today, this being the section behind the cameraman up to Ringway Queens which has now made the road a dead end. The Drill Hall which was the headquarters of the 7th Royal Warwickshire Regiment Territorial Force, became a place for dancing to Big Bands after the last War. It was demolished only a few years ago, now being a car park. The new Co-op store is now the other side of Croft Road.

Rudge Whitworth Scouts c1928 (Unknown)

This group of Scouts seen leaving the Rudge Whitworth Works are walking down Trafalgar Street with Meadow Street to the left behind the cameraman. It would appear that as some are too young to be workers that probably they are workers and their sons away for a week at camp during the holidays. At this time the workers were making their name building motorcycles, the name 'Rudge' still being a name to conjure with in vintage racing circles. The works were recently demolished without any future use of the site being discussed, and is now ripe for over development!

Peace July 19th 1919 (Unknown)

After the ending of the Great War on 11th November 1918, the Government decided that on Saturday 19th July the following year a Peace Day would be celebrated. In Coventry these celebrations started with the combined Sunday Schools massing in Pool Meadow at 9.45am to sing hymns followed by a march around the City. At 3pm a Pageant gathered at the Barracks Square before also marching round the City. In the evening at 10pm a simultaneous Grand Firework Display was held at Spencer Park, Radford Recreation Ground and Stoke Green. In this view taken from Hertford Square looking towards Rudge Road, the local residents can be seen gathering to hold their own celebrations. The Rudge Whitworth building, later GEC can be seen in the background.

Peace Riots Broadgate 1919 (HHT)

Coventry Railwaymens strike 1919 (Unknown)

Unfortunately after the peace celebrations ended, riots broke out in the city centre as it was thought that some of the larger shops were German owned. Dunn's next to the Kings Head Hotel and several other shops in Broadgate and Cross Cheaping had windows broken. The riots came to an end after three nights when the crowd was repeatedly charged by the police. As crowds were then prevented from assembling in Broadgate after 9pm, further violence did not occur. Later, in September the Railwaymen had a strike and although this was of short duration, as a consequence, food rationing, ended after the war, was re-imposed. This was one of several strikes due to the hardship caused by nearly 6000 unemployed in the city. The top view taken during the peace riots shows shops boarded up in Broadgate, Salmon & Glucksteine to the right being on the corner of High Street. The lower view is looking up Warwick Road from the junction of St Patrick's Road, with Lansdowne Place and the entrance to the Railway Goods Depot to the right.

Spon Street 1911 (Unknown)

Spon Street 1911 (Unknown)

Both of these postcards show the Coventry Sunday Schools King George V Coronation Day procession. They were taken at the same time and are both included as they show Spon Street from outside the 'Shakspeare Inn' in each direction. In the top view to the right of the Shakspeare without the E is court 7, then before the works entrance to Rotherhams, at no. 19 is M. Nicks Provision Dealer. Just out of the picture to the right is the 'Old Windmill'. The 'Shakspeare' has since been refaced and the buildings to the right have been demolished. The bottom picture shows to the left of the 'Shakspeare', Alexander Edward's Watch & Clock repairers, followed by the 'Board Vaults' then after court 6 the 'Recruiting Sergeant'. This latter pub closed in 1928, has been much altered and is now known as 'Tudor House'. On the corner of Queen Victoria Road the tall building is the 'Plough Hotel' which was bombed in the last War, Alexander Edwards the jewellers now being in a rebuilt shop on this site.

Hill Street c1913 (A&G Taylor)

Although this view is still recognisable today, with Bond's Hospital to the right and the Tower of St John's Church showing over the roof, nothing now remains of the left hand side of the street. The sign is over the "Newdigate Arms' with Bond Street being to the left of the children in the foreground. Further down on the left was the "White Swan Hotel" on the spot now occupied by Bond's Court. The street then curved round to the left into Fleet Street at the point where Corporation Street would be built in later years.

Fleet Street c1910 (Unknown)

This could almost be the same coach and horses seen outside the 'Three Tuns Hotel' (Page 7), but on this occasion it looks a wet day with puddles in the street. The occupants all have their raincoats on, and obviously hope the day will brighten. St John's Church can be seen to the right. The trees in the middle of Fleet Street are of interest. The Grocers and Wine & Spirit Merchants seen to the left would in later years become Allwoods Atkins & Turton.

Fleet Street c1905 (Unknown)

This view is from the bottom of Smithford Street, looking into Fleet Street with the tram approaching having just passed St John's Church on the right. The 'City Arms Hotel' can be seen on the right, the other side of West Orchard, with Gibney's Wonderful Shoe Hospital on this side. These premises were later demolished, the pre-war Co-op store being built on this site. The 'Old Baths Hotel' is just out of the picture to the left. This area was cleared in 1959, the C&A Store and the bottom of the precinct now being here.

Old Baths Hotel c1910 (Unknown)

Situated at 35 Smithford Street, the 'Old Baths Hotel', which is known to have existed at least 75 years before this picture was taken, finally closed when Smithford Street was redeveloped. Mr. H. Hewitt is seen here proudly standing in front of his premises; the sign above advertising his noted home brewed ales, at 3d, 4d, 5d & 6d per Quart. These premises were used by carriers conveying passengers to and from Allesley and Meriden. Good stabling was also offered, the entrance to the yard at the rear of the premises being seen to the left. Another view can be seen on page 11 of Volume 1.

Well Street Sunday School, Easter 1913 (Waterman)

Despite the inscription on the card this picture was taken in Chapel Street, its junction with Well Street is just behind the photographer. The houses at the end of the street are in Lamb Street which bears off to the left. Well Street Congregational chapel was built in 1827 and gradually expanded over the years so that it fronted both Well and Chapel Streets. The Sunday School was one of these extensions, built in 1850. It regularly took part in the mass meeting of Sunday Schools in Pool Meadow each Easter; the 1913 meeting is commemorated in this picture. By the time of the photograph this area was one of the poorest and most overcrowded in Coventry where large families filled the narrow courts behind the street frontages.

Well Street c1910 (Unknown)

This view is looking into Well Street with The Burges behind the cameraman. The lady on the left is standing in the doorway of the 'Rose Inn' with the 'Old Waggon & Horses' next door. As the picture depicts a Pub outing, the participants could be regulars from these two establishments. When the coaches move off on their journey they will pass 'The Wine Lodge' on the right hand corner of Well Street and The Burges. Further down Well Street on the right is the entrance into Chapel Street, where the top view was taken. The poster on the wall is for Singer's Sewing Machine Shop at 33 Fleet Street.

The Burges c1913 (TH Co)

Matterson Huxley & Watson c1926 (Unknown)

Although the top postcard indicates The Burges, we are in Cross Cheaping, The Burges not beginning until Comleys Furniture Shop seen on the left in the distance. In the row of shops between the entrance into West Orchard seen to the left and Comley's is the premises of Matterson Huxley & Watson shown below. Although the shop front is in itself a wonderful display of cutlery and plated ware, behind the shop was one of the most industrial areas of Coventry. In the area bounded by Cross Cheaping, The Burges, Well Street and West Orchard were grouped the Vulcan Foundry, the Lion Foundry and Iron Works, several Ribbon Works including Victoria Mills together with the Meteor and Albion Bicycle and Tricycle Works. Starting about 1874 Matterson Huxley & Watson began buying these works as they became available. By the time of this advertising postcard, Matterson's had become one of the biggest suppliers and manufacturers of ironware in the Midlands. Even though badly damaged by bombing the works continued until the area was redeveloped in the early 1950's. The West Orchard development is now on this site. Matterson's although not now in manufacture still continue business in their other premises in Hales Street.

Hales Street c1912 (Unknown)

Chas Shadwell & Hippodrome Orchestra. c1933 (Clayton)

It would appear that the boys on the left of this picture are on their way to the Swanswell Pool, as one of them has a fishing net in his hand. They are just passing the entrance into New Buildings on the left, with the entrance into St Agnes Lane just behind the lamppost on the right. It is interesting to think that at that time, behind the wall on the left, was the Cattle Market, whereas today this is the busy corner of Trinity Street and Fairfax Street. The Opera House can just be seen behind the open top Tram no. 43 approaching, which is advertising Hansons Pianos. The New Hippodrome, now Gala Clubs Bingo Hall, was built on the area to the right in 1937. The Mayor of Coventry Alderman A.H. Barnacle carried out the Opening Ceremony on Monday November 1st. William (Bill) Pethers was the leader of the Hippodrome Orchestra at that time. Previously Charles Shadwell who went on to BBC Radio fame had been the leader of the Old Hippodrome Orchestra. On the lower postcard he is seen leading the Orchestra on the stage of the Old Hippodrome, the postcard being signed, 'Sincerely yours Charles M Shadwell.'

Chas. Shadwell & Hippodrome Orchestra, Coventry.

White Street c1907 (Jackson)

This would appear to be another pub outing, the regulars lined up in their Sunday best, ready for the start, being outside the Sir Thomas White Hotel. The publican at the time F.W. Foster is obviously very proud that he can offer Phillips & Marriott prize medal Ales and Stout. The coaches are standing in White Street, with Norton Street to the rear. Swanswell Pool is to the right.

Empire Day, Wheatley Street School 1912 (Waterman)

At the time of this picture Wheatley Street School was less than twenty years old. It was opened in 1893 as a boys and girls infant school. Empire Day on May 24th was an important annual event, a civic dignitary with regalia around his neck, is addressing the crowd. The gathering is in the school playground with Ford Street behind the cameraman. The school had a chequered career, the boys being transferred to John Gulson in 1936 and the girls to Lyng Hall in 1954. At that time it became Priory Secondary Modern School but by the early 1970's had become Sidney Stringer School and Community College. It was demolished in the mid 1980's.

Ford Street c1907 (ER)

This rather faded view of one of Coventry's Victorian residential streets shows a pleasant, not to say elegant, face to an area that has now completely disappeared. The view taken from the White Street end of Ford Street, shows Priory Street crossing in the middle distance. Two buildings on the right are worthy of note, the Art School just in the picture with Trinity Schools behind the photographer. Although it is difficult to see the tram lines due to the poor road condition, the poles with long arms carrying the overhead wires to power the trams are clearly shown. This area was a victim of the ring road development, being just north of the present Pool Meadow bus station.

Lower Ford Street c1912 (Unknown)

With Coventry being a booming City at the time, at the heart of the cycle and motorcycle industry, this postcard is included to show a typical factor of that period. Thomas. L. Prentice had his premises at 145 Lower Ford Street and is shown proudly standing in the doorway, with a Triumph Motorcycle and a selection of cycles on offer. In 1919 these premises became part of Sherbourne Plating when Thomas moved to 140 Far Gosford Street.

Coventry Sunday Schools Coronation Day 1911 (Waterman)

Triumph Co Ltd. c1912 (WY)

The coronation of George V on Thursday June 22nd 1911 was celebrated in Coventry by a Godiva Procession. As part of the proceedings Coventry's Sunday Schools put on their traditional parade through the streets as they normally did at Easter. And also, as Easter, they displayed their massed ranks in Pool Meadow (in this instance 24,000 of them!) before the parade. This was the natural arena for the gathering of any procession in Coventry. One side, to the East, was formed by the Public Baths and Spencer & Co, slay and harness manufacturers in Priory Street, as shown in the picture. In the lower picture, still in Priory Street but looking in the opposite direction, we can now just see the brick fence posts of The Public Baths down on the right. The notice on the premises this side indicating Turkish Baths. On the opposite side of the street the main premises of the Triumph Cycle Co Ltd were situated. Very few of the workers seen leaving the premises would appear to have bicycles, possibly due to the average wage at that time being £1.15.0 (£1.75) per week, whereas the Triumph sales catalogue for that year indicates bicycles from £6.17.6 (£6.88) and motorcycles from £48.15.0 (£48.75).

Priory Street c1912 (Unknown)

This further view of Priory Street is included to show the entrance into New Street on the right. To give an indication of the position of this street, the railings on the left are around St Michael's Church, which in 1918 became The Cathedral. Opposite New Street is the entrance into St. Michael's Avenue. Further down Priory Street on the left can be seen the Triumph Cycle Co. Ltd.

New Street c1912 (Unknown)

This view is looking from New Street towards Priory Street with the entrance into St Michael's Avenue on the opposite side. The gable jutting out over the pavement on the right at the end is seen in the upper picture. The spire of Holy Trinity Church can be seen over the roof. In 1955, New Street, which had mainly survived the bombing and still containded sixty-five buildings, mainly timber framed, was cleared to make way for the Polytechnic, now Coventry University.

Cox Street c1906 (ER)

Taken from the corner of Godiva Street, looking towards Jordan Well, the "Old Star" can be seen on the left, the proprietor at the time being Mrs Ellen Dutson. On the right a water pump can be seen on the pavement at the corner of New Street and just beyond the general dealer is the "Robin Hood Inn." A little further up at the corner of Freeth Street, it can be seen that Waters Oyster Bar are offering blue point oysters at one shilling per score (5p for twenty).

Much Park Street c1912 (Waterman)

This picture postcard shows a view looking down Much Park Street towards Jordan Well with the entrance gate of Whitefriars on the right. Next to the gate it can be seen that I. Greaves the proprietor is offering good lodging for working men only. Just past the lamp post on the left is "The Greyhound" with the large building beyond being Phillips & Marriott's Midland Brewery. On the other side of Jordan Well, The Empire Meat Company can be seen. With the exception of "The Greyhound" and Whitefriars Gate all of the remainder has gone. The new Crown and Country Court building has recently been built on the left.

Gosford Street c1924 (Dania)

Collins, Broker c1916 (Unknown)

Although this postcard indicates Gosford Street, the photographer was standing in Jordan Well. The small street on the left is Freeth Street with the policeman standing at the intersection of Cox Street and Whitefriars Street; Gosford Street then begins. The building on the left with the crossed timbers is McCutchion's fish merchants, with on the other side of Freeth Street, Frank Snape pork butchers. The "Sir Colin Campbell", just seen on the far right hand corner of Whitefriars Street, with a few buildings beyond, are all that now remains of this scene. Typical of many premises in Gosford Street, Collins, Broker and Furniture dealer seen in the lower picture, eventually fell to pre-war re-development. At the time of this picture postcard it was next door to the Hotchkiss Factory (Page 19 Volume 1), but when this factory was enlarged in the early 1930's it disappeared. At that time the original Hotchkiss works had become Morris Motors Engines Branch. Under the archway, a chest of drawers and other items of pine furniture, which are todays' antiques, are being offered new.

Gulson Road c1906 (ER)

Although the cottages seen in this view, known as Craven Terrace, still exist today they are hardly recognisable without the railings which give them here a rural appearance. At the time they stood in isolation at the Binley Road end of Gulson Road which a few years earlier was known as Brick Kiln Lane. Now, they are sandwiched between other terraced houses, the other side of the road has been built up, and the footpath which ran from the small building on the left to London Road has now become St Margaret Road. Swinton Insurance now stands on the corner of these two roads.

Charterhouse Road c1928 (Teesee)

This road was one of several built on the south side of Gulson Road not long after the top picture was taken. It was called Charterhouse Road as it was constructed on the footpath which ran from Gulson Road, near the site of Emma's Well, to the Charterhouse, off London Road. The view is looking towards Gulson Road, with David Road on the right. Taken from the intersection with Northfield Road, the picture shows on the left, the premises of John Waters, who was not only a haulier but supplied Power Petrol at that time.

Martyrs Memorial, Park Road c1910 (Unknown)

Park Road c1908 (Harvey Barton)

Fortunately the Martyrs Memorial, unveiled in a blaze of glory by the Lord Mayor on Thursday 15th September 1910, still survives not far from where it was originally erected. The monument commemorates the burning at the stake of eleven Coventry men and women between 1510 and 1555. The Mayor, Alderman Lee, did not seem to feel that it was necessary for him to know too much about his subject matter. In his speech he stated *"What was the reason for their martyrdom? Were they political or religious, scientific or philosophical martyrs? I must confess I do not know...."* In fact they were religious martyrs who were not prepared to reject their particular interpretation of the Christian faith at a time when England's rulers vacillated between forms of Roman Catholicism and Protestantism. This view taken at the moment of the unveiling is looking up Park Road. The second view of Park Road looking up towards the point where the memorial was to be built gives an uninterrupted view of the Chocolate Factory, later to become Swift Motor and Cycle Work in Quinton Road. Park Road was one of a number set out in this area in the early part of this century to provide accommodation for the growing middle classes of the city.

Bulkington Road c1927 (Teesee)

Known to some as Hawkesbury Lane, this is a view looking towards Bulkington just north of the junction with Lenton's Lane. The pub was demolished soon after this photograph was taken and replaced by one retaining the original name of the Old Crown. The bakers trap was owned by Topp's Bakery whose premises were near the canal bridge, a few hundred yards further south. Inevitably newer buildings have replaced the countryside flanking the road beside the trap.

Alderman's Green Road c1927 (Teesee)

The distinctive houses on the right still stand, part of a development by the local Co-op store that stood on the opposite side of Co-operative Street, the entrance to which is just beyond the furthest house on the right. To locals this will indicate that the view is a north facing one, close to the heart of the village. Most of the cottages on the left have now been demolished, some in the 1930's and others as late as the 1970's. These are very typical of the mainly nineteenth century free-for-all development of roadside housing in the area. Though, in places, the twentieth century developments don't seem to be any more organised.

136-6   HALL GREEN ROAD

Hall Green Road c1927 (Teesee)

Thanks to the stream not being culverted and the wooden fence having been replaced by an identical concrete one, fixing the location of this view is not as difficult as it might otherwise be. The recent development of Pauline Avenue to the left confirms that this shows the north end of Hall Green Road looking towards Hall Green itself. The trees have gone, replaced by a hedge flanking the stream concealing the post-war housing estate developed on the fields behind. Where the road bends to cross this stream, the turn is so gentle today as to be almost unnoticeable, yet at the early part of the century this immediate area was named after the crossing point, Hall Green Bridge.

136-9   WYKEN POOL

Wyken Pool c1927 (Teesee)

It is tempting to suggest that the proximity of Wyken Pool to the many mine workings in the area might suggest that its origins are man-made. This may have contributed to its present size but the evidence would indicate that this is not the only reason. Most mineworking in the area started in the late sixteenth century or later but reference was first made in 1545 to the existence of a pool. Whatever the case it has been a popular recreation spot for many years though sadly boating has not been a regular feature for some time. Even the boathouse shown here has now gone. It was occupied at the time of the picture by the Rose family who made a living by hiring out boats and angling placements. It looks as if the photographer was in a boat to get this view. The planners have done well to preserve this spot and develop it as an even more attractive recreational resource.

Allesley Village c1906 (Frederic Lewis)

The photographer was standing on the footpath leading to the parish church of All Saints when he took this shot looking along a very narrow Birmingham Road towards Meriden. On the left the fencing has been removed and the wall built higher but the "Rainbow Inn" seen just beyond and the remainder of the buildings look much as today. The two telegraph poles, and the tree on the left have long since disappeared, the entrance to the Allesley Hotel now being on the left where the girls and cart are standing. Thank goodness Allesley was declared a conservation area in 1968.

Staircase Lane c1910 (Blakeman & Saville)

The tranquillity of Allesley in the early part of this century is clearly shown on this postcard. The view is taken looking away from the village towards Brownshill Green, the cart coming towards the cameraman is possibly from Brownshill Green Farm. Although this Lane became a popular walk it has been, to a certain extent, ruined by the relief road across the Coundon Wedge, now cutting it in two.

Butts Lane c1932 (Teesee)

It would seem that the photographer who originally took this picture possibly got his notes mixed up as this is of course Butcher's Lane. Sidney Harris the butcher has opened his shop as the second door on the left is open. The canopy over the shop has now been removed and two garages have been built on the end, but otherwise the left hand side of the Lane is still recognisable. On the right the barn has been demolished and an electricity sub-station has been built together with an entrance into 62/64 Birmingham Road, a sympathetically restored house built about 1580.

The *Paybody Convalescent Home c1932 (Teesee)*

This building, originally known as "The Elms", is shown soon after it became a Convalescent Home, being presented to the Coventry and District Crippled Childrens Guild by Thomas Paybody in 1929. The building now looks a poor version of the original building shown, since it recently closed. By being left to decay there is a danger that vandals will do the developers work for them. This will then release this valuable site on the corner of the relief road for other uses.

ALLESLEY OLD ROAD.

Allesley Old Road c1926 (Unknown)

Broad Lane c1928 (G&Co)

It is hard to believe that today this point on the Allesley Old Road is at the Grayswood Avenue junction. The car on the bridge to the left is on its way towards Coventry, the bridge on which the children are standing carries a footpath further along called Guphill Lane towards Whoberley Hall. The Hall stood, where today, Lyndale Road meets Glendower Avenue. The footpath from Hearsall Common to Whoberley Hall is now called Guphill Avenue. In the lower picture the corner of Glendower Avenue and Broad Lane can be seen. Although very little altered from today, at that time Glendower Avenue had only just been opened to motor traffic, previously being only a footpath to Whoberley Hall and Allesley. Broad Lane, beyond where the Fletchamstead Highway would be built six years later, only being a country lane. Buses were however using the route as Motor Bus Stage is indicated on the lamp-post where the lady and girl are awaiting a bus into the City. The Newsagent G.H. Hawthorn can be seen with S. North, Broad Lane Supply Stores next door.

BROAD LANE, COVENTRY.

Allesley Old Road c1939 (Richards)

Queensland Avenue c1927 (Teesee)

Both of these postcard views have one thing in common in that when they were taken Four Pounds Avenue did not exist at this end. The top view is looking towards the City, with Queensland Avenue on the right, H.W. Hawthorn Newsagent & Confectioner being on the corner. The cottages on the left were demolished when Four Pounds Avenue was completed after the War. Until then it had only been completed up to Lake View Road, just a footbridge continuing over the River Sherbourne. The bottom view, looking down Queensland Avenue, shows a profusion of mature trees where the Safeway Superstore now stands, on the other side of Allesley Old Road. The road crossing half way down is Abercorn Road, with R.J. Grimston Grocer on the left hand corner. Just behind the cameraman on the right is Craven Street.

The Atherstone Hunt, Craven Arms 1914 (Unknown)

This meet of the Atherstone Hunt was held on March 13th 1914. It is a scene unlikely to be acted out on this spot again. At the time the Cravens of Coombe Abbey owned all the land around and would not need to seek permission to hold a wide ranging hunt. It is also likely that in this picture is represented most of the wealthy tenants and neighbours of the Cravens upon whose land they were most likely to chase any foxes. The Craven Arms in the background would be a most appropriate place to pass round a warming stirrup cup as can be seen on the right.

Brinklow Road c1927 (Teesee)

One element of this view still exists and that is the thatched building on the right that was the village school up to 1913. It has had a chequered history losing its thatched roof along the way. It is now a restaurant. The thatched cottages on the left have also gone, though they were revived after this picture and re-thatched. The cottage on the left is also advertising the sale of sweets and drinks, which is not just meant for the villagers but for those from Coventry who made this part of a popular route for week-end walks out of town. The road on the left is Clifford Bridge Road and the one on the right is Brinklow Road.

Craven Stores, Brandon Road 1936 (Walker)

Just round the corner from the Craven Arms is the garage which replaced the smithy and, continues to function today as a petrol station. Over the same period these four shops were built to serve the demands of the growing community. Despite their apparent specialism a whole range of services and products could be supplied such as meat, haberdashery, hairdressing, film processing, holidays etc. The newspaper hoardings provide fascinating information, announcing the new Triumph models for 1937, that Foreign Minister Eden ordered to rest by doctors and rather enigmatically, in the Daily Mirror, "Women Jeer Girl Saved In Triple Drowning".

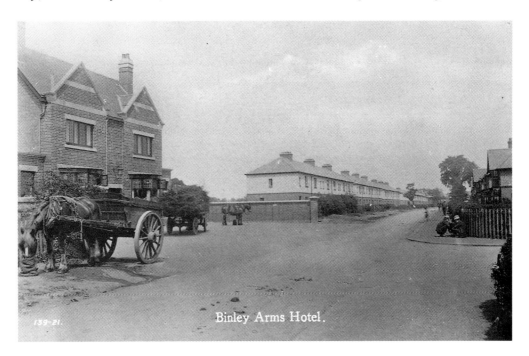

Binley Arms Hotel, c1927 (Teesee)

This charming photograph of the pub with the carthorse eating from its nose bag shows the view looking east toward Binley village along Willenhall Lane. Only recently opened at the time of the picture, the first landlord, William Farley, had been appointed licensee in March 1926. It was a shrewd move by Marstons, the owners, as all those thirsty miners over the road had at least a mile to go to the nearest pub. The only surprising fact is that no one had opened a pub earlier as the colliery had been open almost twenty years. The building remains substantially unaltered today, (though now named "The Binley"), yet the details of modern street furniture and decoration, not to say the ever present motor car mean that this still records a scene of the Coventry we have lost.

Clifford Bridge Road c1936 (Walker)

Housing for the miners of Binley colliery was originally based around the pithead on Willenhall Lane, but later accommodation was built alongside Clifford Bridge Road. These still flank the road from Mill Lane to the bridge over the Sowe. At this time the road was the responsibility of Warwickshire County Council and it seems clear that the normal standards of drainage and verging were not to be applied to this development yet!

Brandon Road, Binley c1936 (Walker)

For a fairly quiet Warwickshire backwater Brandon Road has made up for its sleepy past in post-war developments. The construction of houses on the left, pre-war, did bring a suburban touch to the area but some of the ex-Coombe Abbey estate workers cottages opposite date back almost a couple of centuries earlier. By 1960 Binley Park Comprehensive School had been built on 44 acres behind these cottages. A few years earlier agricultural land nearby had begun to be developed as an industrial estate, which grew further on the site of the local redundant colliery. Today Binley Park has also closed and the whole area between this scene and the newly opened Eastern By-pass is to be devoted to commercial and industrial use.

Canley Water Falls c1912 (Waterman)

Prior Deram Walk c1939 (Richards)

These two views are connected in their way. The first, chosen as very few postcards showing buildings in old Canley exist, is of Canley Brook. After crossing Watery Lane, seen on page 86 of Volume I, the brook crossed fields where due to the changing ground levels these waterfalls existed. In 1936, the section of the Fletchamstead Highway was commenced from Canley Road to the railway bridge at Fletchamstead and this section of the brook was re-developed, now being under the Highway. This development did also bring about the building of modern Canley, when Sherriff Avenue, Prior Deram Walk and the surrounding roads were laid out. The bottom view shows the group of shops on the corner of Prior Deram Walk and D'Aubney Road. Clews Canley Stores and Newsagents has a newsboard outside announcing 'Britain Warns Hitler'.

Torrington Avenue c1939 (Richards)

Standard Aero Works c1939 (Richards)

The photographer who took these pictures only had to turn around to take the second view, as they were taken at the same time. They must also have been taken on the same day as the picture of Prior Deram Walk on the previous page, as a newsboard saying 'Britain Warns Hitler' is also outside R.C. Blockley's Newsagents. The next shop is Mrs Arnett's fried fish saloon, with on the opposite side of Torrington Avenue, Coventry Swaging Company later to become the Torrington Company. Torrington Avenue at this time terminated at Templar Avenue, a footpath continuing past Fletchamstead Hall to Station Avenue at Tile Hill. The bottom view of the Standard Aero Works shows the cycle track on the Fletchamstead Highway not yet surfaced. Although this portion of the Standard Motor Company Works (originally built in 1937 as a 'Shadow Factory' to produce aero engines) still exists as part of the Rover Company, the part which was Standard Spares and Service has recently been demolished. This corner of Tile Hill Lane is to become yet another superstore. One of the trees recently cut down can be seen over the factory roof.

Tile Hill Lane c1939 (Richards)

Another picture taken at the same time as those on the opposite page shows the Standard Picture House not long after it was first opened. The interesting thing is that one of the compilers of this book, could have been inside at the time, as his father's Pontiac car reg no. BOX 667 is shown on the left. Although a hairdressers and other shops exist today, only the Standard Stores in the small part jutting out to the right of the Cinema existed then. Barclays Bank on the opposite corner would not be built for another twenty years. The island complete with ornate lamp standard and "Keep Left" bollards is worthy of note.

Fir Tree Avenue c1931 (Teesee)

Lime Tree Estate was constructed in the late 1920's not only to house the increasing population, but to accommodate people whose houses in the Well Street area were demolished for the building of Corporation Street. Fir Tree Avenue, seen here from the intersection with Beech Tree Avenue looking towards Elm Tree Avenue, is still "Unadopted" at this time, the road still being poorly surfaced with no kerbs yet existing.

Job's Lane c1936 (Unknown)

This view is looking towards Broad Lane from a point opposite Lime Tree Avenue, the entrance into which, can be seen on the right. The surface of the Lane is still unmade without kerbs, and very few lamp-posts are evident. On the right hand side a detached house has now been built between the first and second pair of houses and further on Ballingham Close now exists. On the left hand side very few houses had been erected, but now this side is fully built up with Lawley Close just past the lamp post.

Cross Roads c1930 (Unknown)

This view of the cross roads at Tile Hill has Tanners Lane leading to Berkswell stretching away beyond the man. Banner Lane is to the right with the roof of Tanyard Farm showing through the trees. To the left is Station Road leading to Tile Hill Railway Station. On the far left corner is where the Midland Bank is situated today, the "Bell Inn" being further to the left on the same side.

Tile Hill c1923 (G&Co)

It is hard to believe that this is a view looking towards the cross roads from Station Road with Banner Lane disappearing into the distance. The only clue is the building with the three gables seen on the left which today is the general store and off-licence. Further along on the same side is the "Bell Inn". Where the small pathway is on the immediate left Rex Close is now situated, with modern houses on the opposite side of Station Road, on the site of the Tile Hill Mission Room.

Tile Hill Cottage c1923 (G&Co)

Visitors to the Midland Sports Centre for the Disabled at Tile Hill would not realise that this cottage still exists today on the opposite side to the railway station. When the picture was taken it was in open countryside. Today the tidy garden is now overgrown and the cottage can hardly be seen from Cromwell Lane, which was named after this cottage. The year on the postcard is incorrect; 'Cromwell Cottage 1653" being indicated over the door! The large pine tree on the right still exists, but double gates have now replaced the single wooden gate and path leading to the front door.

Tile Hill c1923 (G&Co)

Nailcote Avenue c1932 (Teesee)

Both of these views show Nailcote Avenue, the top picture capturing the build up of housing which had begun whilst Tile Hill was still a true village. It would be a further five years before it became part of Coventry. The big detatched house on the left, together with a similar house further up appear to have been built for some time, but the bungalows are of more modern design. It is interesting to see that the house further up on the left has an advert for 'Lyons Tea' on the side, so it could well have been a shop at this time. Behind the cameraman, to the right, a small pathway led to Conway Avenue which is not named today, but maps of the period show it as Cross Road. The bottom picture although taken after Tile Hill became part of Coventry, still shows the road unadopted and in poor condition. It would not be until after the War that this condition was rectified. The bungalow seen on the right is on the corner of Duggins Lane, Ye Olde Blacksmiths Shop, shown on page 89 of Volume I being on the opposite side of the lane.

Under the spreading *walnut* tree
The village smithy stands
AT BROWNSHILL GREEN, COUNDON.   SIDWELL, MERIDEN.

Smithy, Brownshill Green c1905 (Sidwell)

The blacksmith, Joe Sparrow, can be seen by the side of his forge. The business survived into the sixties but the premises were soon taken over by the expanding garage that can still be seen there today. The house itself exists but is no longer a good example of sleepy country living. It has been almost swamped by the roundabout at the northern exit of the Coundon Wedge Road, the road surface having been raised above the surrounding ground level.

Rialto Picture Theatre c1930 (Unknown)

Opened in 1928 the Rialto was one of a number of suburban cinemas opened at this time to serve the needs of the new estates and satisfy the interest created by the introduction of the 'talkies'. It was taken over by the Odeon cinema group in 1940 but was soon to fall victim to a German bombing raid. A similar victim was Barclays Bank seen in the background on the opposite corner of the Barker Butts, Moseley Avenue junction. Its style, however, was very similar to Lloyds bank which did survive on the east side.

Earlsdon Street c1906 (Slapoffski)

Earlsdon Street c1926 (Teesee)

Although only twenty years separate these pictures much had changed in that period. In the top picture the 'City Arms' is the original building, with the Earlsdon Working Mens Club on the opposite side with a row of cottages on this side of Moor Street and the 'Royal Oak' on the far corner. At this time nothing would have existed on the corners of Albany Road behind the cameraman. By the time of the lower picture, Earlsdon Library and the Methodist Church would have been built on these corners. The view in the lower picture is looking towards the Library with Providence Street on the right. The tram has Jordan Well on the indicator board so it has come via Smithford Street. In later years when Smithford Street had become too congested, the route to Earlsdon was Hertford Street and Queens Road. The lack of motor vehicles parked in the street is far different to today's situation.

Mayfield Road c1912 (Waterman)

This postcard view of early Earlsdon is taken from Mayfield Road looking towards Earlsdon Avenue, with G.E. Seeney's Newsagents on the left, on the corner of Mickleton Road. As well as advertising papers together with weeklys such as "Home Chat" and "Boys Friend", farm fed pork together with home cured ham and bacon is also indicated on the window. On the other side of Earlsdon Avenue, 'Holly Bank' with a monkey puzzle and other mature conifers in front can be seen. Sadly, it has become a victim of subsequent redevelopment.

Kensington Road c1913 (TH Co)

The parents of the children seen in this picture, would have moved into their newly completed homes only a few years before. This area originally known as Earlsdon Gardens was developed mainly by the Newcombe Brothers of Market Harborough, the whole area between Chapelfields and Earlsdon being completed by the time of this postcard. The view with Westwood Road just out of the picture to the left is looking towards Earlsdon Avenue North. Most of the railings have long since disappeared and the wall against which the girl is leaning has been opened up to allow a garage to be built.

Palmerston Road c1913 (Waterman)

Laying the Foundation Stone, Palmerston Road Church Hall 1913 (Waterman)

The picture of Palmerston Road shows a strange meeting ground between the contrasting housing developments in the area with affluent Earlsdon on the right and working class terraced Earlsdon on the left. It was also the location for a familiar event in the expanding Coventry of the early twentieth century; the building of a new church. Earlsdon, which had previously been served by St Thomas's in the Butts, was in as much need as any of the suburbs. The second picture shows the foundation stone was being laid at the site of what is now the present church hall but was originally built as temporary church. The ceremony was performed on Monday evening, 16th June 1913. The picture shows the congregation singing the hymn "Christ is made the sure Foundation", shortly before the women in the centre of the picture, the Hon Mrs Baillie, formally tapped the stone into place. The building was opened in December 1913, less than six months after this picture was taken, with spaces for 300 people. The original idea that a proper church would be built at a later date alongside this building was not carried through.

Unveiling the Cenotaph, Spender Park 1919 (Sylvester)

Spencer Avenue c1920 (Ralphs Real Photos)

To the eagle-eyed, a small stone acting as a reminder of the Cenotaph unveiled on 12th October 1919 can still be seen in the Dalton Road corner of the park. The latter was erected eight years after the ceremony depicted in the first postcard, when the City's war memorial was unveiled in Memorial Park. At the same time an oak was planted that had been grown from an acorn gathered at Verdun in 1916. This original ceremony in 1919 was Coventry's first attempt at a memorial to its dead from the First World War. Despite being performed in very poor weather the ceremony was reportedly attended by thousands who gathered after a procession from Pool Meadow. They collected the Mayor and sword and mace bearers on the way past the Council House. The Mayor, who performed the unveiling ceremony, referred to the cenotaph, not unkindly, as *"quite a homemade affair"* as it was constructed of wood in the form of an obelisk surmounted by a cross painted in black and white. It had been designed, built and paid for by discharged soldiers. Clearly a larger memorial had not been planned at this stage as it was hoped that the wooden cenotaph would simply be replaced by an identical stone one. The name Spencer also features in the name of the road passing by the park, shown in the second picture. Both were named after David Spencer, a Coventry Draper and Wool Merchant. As well as presenting the land for the park in 1882, six years before his death, he was a generous contributor to numerous other local charitable causes.

Albany Road 1904 (Unknown)

Although no-one was injured this accident drew crowds from all over the city to see the four railway carriages which had rolled down the bank on to the Albany Road. The accident occurred during the early hours of 2nd July, when carriages, were were being assembled together, for an outing to the seaside. This picture would have been taken days later, as it was found necessary to build a track down the bank to enable the carriages to be pulled up, one at a time, by a locomotive. Here the cable has been connected, and the pull is about to commence. The bridge over Albany Road is just to the left, with the 'Albany Hotel' at the bottom of Broomfield Road, to the left of the cameraman.

The Regent Rollerdrome, Albany Road c1936 (Unknown)

At the side of the Railway embankment at the bottom of Broomfield Road is the entrance into what was Butts Mews, where several buildings stood. At the time of this advertising postcard one of these buildings was Coventry's Skating Rendezvous, with an adjacent building being Neale's Engineering Company. The building shown after the last War became Neals's Ballroom which before being destroyed by fire had become one of Coventry's leading meeting places for young dancers.

Old Dyers Arms Benevolent Society c1913 (Waterman)

This charming scene captured outside the "Old Dyers Arms" in Spon Street shows Bill Jackson, assisted by several regulars about to treat the local children to a bread and jam party. The pleasure this annual event gave the children is clearly seen on their faces. Let us hope that a campaign will be mounted to prevent this pub together with the "Black Horse Inn" the other side of the railway arches from being demolished for yet another road widening scheme.

The Butts Cycle Track c1906 (Unknown)

An early cycle meeting about to start at the Butts track which was built in 1879 at a time when Coventry led the world in cycle design and production. The view is looking towards The Butts with Sovereign Row behind the stand to the left. The steeple of St Osburg's Church in Hill Street can be seen to the right. The future of this track now seems very much under threat.

Coventry Technical College c1936 (Teesee)

This view of the Technical College was taken soon after it was opened on December 10th 1935 by HRH the Duke of York, later to become King George VI. During his opening speech the Duke said "After visiting some of the less fortunate towns, it is very cheering to be here in the midst of manufacturing activity and development". It is interesting to see that the tram lines from Queens Road and The Butts turn up Albany Road although later in March 1937 the Earlsdon tram service was replaced by buses.

Aerial View Coventry Technical College 1936 (Midland Air Services)

At the time this picture was taken, it can be seen that although the Technical College is complete, the gymnasium at the rear is still being built. A game is being played on the field, so it would seem that students have already been enrolled, following the opening in the previous December. A tram can be seen on Albany Road between Bedford Street and Brunswick Road. On the other side of The Butts, just to the left of the Technical College roof can be seen Hope Street with Windsor Street a little further to the left with the Summerland Tavern, now the Fob Watch, just beyond. Between The Butts and the Rudge Works can be seen the area of Spon Street, Trafalgar Street, Thomas Street, Moat Street, Rudge Road, Albion Street and Crow Lane completely cleared to enable the Ringway Rudge section of the Ring Road to be built.

Brunswick Road c1906 (ER)

This view of Brunswick Road is looking from Albany Road towards Gordon Street with the chimney of a machine tool company showing over the roofs. This company on the corner of Upper York Street and Queens Road became Alfred Herbert, later Winfray Engineering and is now the Winfray building of the Technical College. The carts in the road are interesting, the one nearest the cameraman having a large dog inside. Behind the cameraman on the other side of Albany Road, next to the cycle track was the cricket ground on which the Technical College would be built in 1935.

The Butts c1927 (Unknown)

This view looking from The Butts towards Queens Road, shows Albany Road on the right and further down on the same side the entrance into Gordon Street. The trees between are in front of St Thomas's Church demolished in 1975. The houses between Gordon Street and Upper York Street remain but are now mainly shop premises. The large gates on the left were to a private house later to become Roach Bros. car dismantlers. The next building became the College Bookshop after the Technical College was built. All of the buildings on this side were demolished and Apollo House now stand on this spot.

51

170—1   COURTAULD'S LTD., COVENTRY

Courtauld's Ltd c1922 (Teesee)

Water Storage Tank Courtauds c1912 (Appleby)

Compared to the picture used in the previous book, Courtaulds has now expanded rapidly based on the success of its revolutionary artificial fibre, Rayon. It was a world player in this market. It seems appropriate that Foleshill, for so long home to a significant ribbon weaving industry should now be the base for this new textile industry. Much of the building shown here was part of that expansion, though at the core is still the original 1904 works. This road junction with Lockhurst Lane is constantly busy today compared to the occasional burst of activity at the change of shifts then, though the view is now softened, not to say obscured by a number of large copper beeches. Sadly, as in much of Foleshill, the roadside trees like the one in the foreground here have not survived. The second picture shows that the workers welfare was catered for even in the midst of all those chemicals! Courtaulds obtained all its own water from bore holes on the site. During breaks this water storage tank in the factory, available in case of fires, was just the place for a bit of discreet bathing for the female labour force. Most are wearing identical club or company costumes.

Foleshill Road c1907 (E.R.)

In general whilst humble cottages and large factories may come and go substantial pubs are a little like the parish church and tend to survive, even if in name only. The Golden Eagle on the right can be seen still in its latest incarnation at the junction with Eagle Street – presumably the former giving its name to the latter. To the left is the entrance to Dubbock, Jones & Co weaving works which spread out behind the cottages up to the canal. Though much has disappeared, the small terrace beyond the pub still survives as do some of the houses beyond the weaving works entrance.

Prince William Henry, Lower Foleshill Road c1927 (Unknown)

A splendid survival from Foleshill's earlier golden age, even today this building is surprisingly similar to this postcard. Yet externally it still gives you the feel for Foleshill's peculiar mixture of rural industry and agriculture. Proprieter W.K. Hollick, landlord for much of the 1920's, stands by the entrance with a woman nearby in front of a weighing machine. Presumably the space invader gadget of its time, the weighing machine was quite a common feature of pubs in the early part of the century. Note the old water pump to the left and the tram tracks in front. The street cobbles are gone today and a lick of paint gives the building a more respectable air, but as one of the more remarkable features of Foleshill's agriculture past it deserves a mention.

St Pauls Road c1912 (Waterman)

This, one of the grander streets of Foleshill, remains substantially the same as it is shown in this view, yet it is in the detail that some of the significant changes can be found. As with so many semi-detached houses of this period where decorative detail overlaps between the two houses a common approach to maintenance is not adopted so that the symmetry of the gable ends is lost, and with it part of the architectural integrity of the street.

Foleshill Hall c1917 (Unknown)

There is a certain contradiction in terms between the industrialist working class image of Foleshill and the image of grand living that this picture conveys. Yet at the time of the First World War there were a number of large houses in this area. Admittedly most were throwbacks to the times when such houses had manorial status over a largely agricultural Foleshill. This hall was originally a manor house and continued to be the centre of a small estate until its conversion into a pub during the First World War. The first landlord, Henry Sutton, took over what was to be known as "Foleshill Olde Hall" pub and hotel in February 1917. The building, quite recently demolished, was to be found along Lythall's Lane on the north east side of the railway bridge.

Station Street East, c1914 (H.H.T.)

Great Heath c1922 (Teesee)

This was one of a number of late nineteenth century streets built simply to provide space for residential development to house the workers of the many factories and workshops being opened in the district. It also continued to provide homes for those who wanted to live outside the city. Like some other early suburban streets of Foleshill the developers tried to add a touch of an 'avenue' feel by planting a few trees, with varying degrees of conviction; sadly the ones here have not survived. Station Street East, as the name suggests, is to the east of Foleshill Road opposite the General Wolf, in the area then commonly known as Great Heath. This was obviously a good enough term to identify the location of the second picture, opposite the entrance to Station Street East, at the corner of Station Street West. Lloyds Bank on the far left still features at this location today. Some tram tracks can be seen to veer across the street towards the location of the first picture. This was part of a failed plan to include Station Street East in the tramway system. As can be seen in the first picture there is no evidence of a tramway, indeed judging from the behaviour of the children very little traffic passed this way, unlike its present role as a rat run between Stoney Stanton Road and the Foleshill Road.

GREAT HEATH, COVENTRY

Primrose Hill Street c1907 (E.R.)

Victoria Street c1906 (Slapoffski)

These two views are back to back shots from the same spot and though taken about the same time they are by different publishers using quite different methods of reproduction. The second is a coloured print made from a photograph and the first is a faded sepia finish sold as an original photographic postcard. The former is normally preferable to the latter, but in this instance the printed version has survived better. The previous book had a view from the other end of Victoria Street. This one is from the town end looking east, showing the Royal Exchange pub, officially in Castle Street. The pub is now a shop. Further along on the right is the rather gothic looking facade of a building since demolished and replaced by the ultra plain shop of Phillips the hardware firm. The view down Primrose Hill Street, into town, follows the line of the tramway with Joseph Sutton butchers to the right and Vine Street to the left. The rather faded chimney rising far above the terrace on the left is that of Wheatley Street Flour Mill. Nearly all the buildings have been demolished over the years with the exception of a few of the houses fifty or so yards down on the right.

Victoria Street c1916 (Coupon Photo Co)

This was how the premises of J. Rollason Fruiterer of 35-37 Victoria Street, looked on Christmas Eve 1916. The chickens, ducks and geese, all have labels on, ready for collection. Boxes and wicker baskets of vegetables together with holly in the road and over the shop blinds complete the scene. The health inspector would not be very happy with this display or Mr. Rollason smoking, but undoubtedly the food would have tasted far better than today.

373-3   KING WILLIAM STREET, COVENTRY

King William Street c1930 (Teesee)

This view taken from the Berry Street end of King William Street is looking towards Victoria Street. The shop on the right is Blackmore's wireless depot with Whitehall, fruiterer, next door. Beyond the standard car the entrance into Clarence Street can be seen. In the far distance the Palladium Picture Theatre can be seen next to the 'Ivy Cottage Inn'. On the left just before Waterloo Street can be seen some of the top shops, a reminder that this area had been an important ribbon weaving centre. On the other side of Waterloo Street the 'New Inn' can be seen.

373—9   VERNON STREET, COVENTRY

Vernon Street c1930 (Teesee)

Berry Street c1930 (Teesee)

The right hand side of the top picture shows the Vernon Street portion of the Vernon Street triangle, formed by buildings contained within Vernon Street, Berry Street and Brook Street. This triangle of sixty-seven cottage homes were erected in the 1850's for Eli Green, a wealthy ribbon manufacturer. A central steam engine provided the power for the shafting to operate the looms in the top shops, the shafting passing from cottage to cottage down the whole length of the buildings. This enabled independent weavers to operate only paying rent on their cottage and the power that they used. This group of buildings, as important to Coventry's industrial history as those built by the Cash brothers at Radford at about the same time, were demolished in the early 1950's.

The top view looking down Vernon Street towards St Peter's Church, seen in the distance, has Ward's the grocers and Alfred Isherwood pork butchers on the left. The shop on the right half way down with the blind down is Oldham's grocers. In the lower view seen from Berry Street looking into King William Street, Hammonds butchers can be seen on the right on the corner of King Edward Road. This picture must have been taken just after the one of King William Street shown on the previous page as the Standard car has moved off and is seen passing Blackmore's wireless shop on the right. It is interesting that at the time of the picture an Eli Green was living at no.23 Berry Street. Who was he?

373—1   BERRY STREET, COVENTRY

Paynes Lane c1934 (Unknown)

The cameraman who took this picture was standing in Paynes Lane, with the tram travelling towards him, turning from Berry Street. The entrance into Primrose Hill Park, can be seen behind the car to the right. The Lodge House to Primrose Hill House can still be seen although the house itself was demolished in 1913. The Lodge has now also been demolished.The route of the tram from Paynes Lane was via Binley Road to the terminus at Uxbridge Avenue, Stoke.

The Binley Oak, Paynes Lane c1913 (Unknown)

There are few reminders left of the early activities of Coventry City FC in this area though all the grounds that they have used so far are nearby. Indeed their present headquarters at Highfield Road is only a couple of streets away from this pub which has inscribed on its front "LATE HEADQUARTERS OF THE COVENTRY CITY F.C." Despite the truth of this statement it is unlikely that this inscription actually existed in reality, but is an advertising sleight of hand requested by the landlord, W J Penn, whose name appears on the front of the postcard. The building itself has a gloriously decorated facade that is still impressive despite the comparatively recent painting over of its original ceramic covering.

Swan Lane, c1919 (Unknown)

Frederick Bird School. c1907 (ER)

This dairyman with his horse and delivery cart are seen leaving the Co-op Dairy premises in Swan Lane. Frederick Bird School can just be seen in the distance behind the rear of the cart. Except for the houses on the other side of the lane, with the roof of the Naval Gunshop of the Ordnance Works showing over the roof of the end house, the appearance is still of a lane. A number of mature trees and the remnants of a field hedge give further proof. Britain's industrial future had passed this way more than a hundred years before, when the Coventry Canal was built. It is still to be found beyond these houses to the right, Newnham Road backing onto the canal. The second picture shows Frederick Bird School in all its glory just two years after it was opened as a mixed infants school. In 1913 separate boys and girls sections were opened, then in 1921 secondary and junior sections were opened. After many changes it eventually became a junior school. As it was considered unsuitable to meet modern educational standards the school was demolished in the mid 1980's, a new one being built in its place. What a pity, a part of the original building could not have been retained for some purpose, to give present students a connection with the past.

45—5   KERESLEY CHURCH   LAWLEDGE, RADFORD P.O.

Keresley Church, c1920 (Teesee)

The Hall Hotel c1950 (Constance Ltd)

Though more a view of the road than a view of St Thomas's, the caption would be even less appropriate today as the church is almost completely hidden by trees. This route out of Coventry has been considered important since medieval times and was turnpiked in 1762, but it has attracted less ribbon development, until this century, than its parish twin, Bennetts Road. The photographer is standing in the entrance to Coundon Hall. By 1948 this private house was now a hotel, shown in the second picture, and although the postcard caption has the house in Keresley it is in fact in Coundon, the boundary between the two running along the Tamworth Road. The rural setting of this view has been preserved by the creation of Coundon Hall Park. The house itself has recently had a rather uncertain commercial existence, no longer in its last incarnation as a steakhouse.

THE HALL HOTEL, KERESLEY, COVENTRY.

Alcock Convalescent Hospital,1925 (Appleby)

After demolishing his old house in Stoke to make way for the Humber factory, William Hillman had this house built as Keresley Hall, just off the east side of the Tamworth Road. After his death the house was bought and converted into a convalescent hospital with the money left from a bequest by a local man, John Alcock. At its opening in 1929 by Countess Haig pride was expressed in the minimal alterations that had been made to the grandeur of the building – if only the same could be said today! In 1968 the hospital closed and became the Royal Court Hotel.

Main Road c1927 (Teesee)

The spire of St Thomas's just showing in the centre of the picture tells us that Main Road is in fact the Tamworth Road looking north out of Coventry, near its junction with Bennetts Road South. Only the cottage seen above the car the other side of High Street, has gone today having been demolished in the 1960's. The terrace on the left has been renovated and the furthest dwelling no longer acts as the police house. The policeman is in fact one of the customers standing by the baker's van. The smart chauffeur, no doubt from one of the large houses in Keresley, stands by a Humber car. He would probably approve of the untidy roadside being tidied up by the pavement and kerbs that stretch along both sides of the road today.

The Jetty c1927 (Teesee)

Remarkably no buildings survive from this compact street scene and would take some discovering today. It is in fact the west end of High Street, near the junction of Bennetts Road South and Tamworth Road, looking towards the latter. The first cottage on the right was at one time the local bakehouse; it together with the rest of the cottages on that side of the road were demolished after the war to be replaced by more spacious housing. Those buildings on the left were demolished in the 1930's around about the time that the street changed its name.

Spring Hill c1927 (Teesee)

Known more commonly as Spingfield Hill at the time, this group of houses is located on Bennett's Road South by the junction with Penny Park Lane. For the moment, the onward march of Coventry's suburbs ends at this point, most old village houses flanking the road south of here have been demolished, but this group remains. None are of a great age, the first cottage on the left was built in the mid nineteenth century for the coachman at Keresley House. Dominating the immediate area would have been Springhill House and farm which was on the right hand side of the road, south of the Penny Park Lane junction. All remnants were cleared away by the 1960's.

Windmill Road c1925 (Teesee)

It takes no great scholar to work out the origin of this road name. Whilst not the highest spot in the area it was obviously sufficiently exposed to make it worthwhile to build a windmill. According to the 1775 enclosure map it would have been located to the north side of the road near where Recreation Road is now found. This view is taken from the junction of Windmill Road Longford Road. The rather gloomy view for many of these houses, as today, is to look out on Foleshill Cemetery to the south side of the road. The large house to the right is in fact the cemetery lodge.

Market Square c1905 (Sidwell)

One of the joys of Longford is the many different little bits of townscape unique to this area, either because they have been demolished elsewhere in the city or they always were peculiar to this part of Coventry. The square, seems to have its origins in the last century to judge from the architecture, but whether they replaced older buildings it is difficult to know. This was the site of Longford Wake, a fair held during the third week of August. Late in the nineteenth century it was moved to a local field, but the custom died out some while ago. Most of these buildings still survive as private homes, though most are now covered in various forms of rendering. The shop on the right has disappeared under the expansion of the Saracens Head. The lack of sensitivity that has allowed the mess of buildings that face these houses is deplorable. It greatly detracts from an otherwise fascinating area.

Woodshires Road c1913 (Waterman)

Station Road c1913 (Waterman)

Woodshires Green was one of the many small hamlets that made up the district north of the town centre. It is now on the margins of the present day city; the boundary with Warwickshire passing within a few hundred yards of the end house shown here. The Coventry and Nuneaton branch railway still cuts it off from Longford, but the building of the houses to the right, in the first decade of this century, filled the last remaining area of open road between it and Longford. The closure of Rowley Lane with the opening of the new link road has brought some peace back to this area. The houses shown in Station Road date from half a century or so earlier. Their pleasant situation alongside the canal does not reflect the life-style of many of their original inhabitants who slaved in the local coalmines between Coventry and Nuneaton. Though known at the time as Station Road, leading as it does to Longford Station, the modern name of Sydnall Road has much more ancient associations with the area. It has been variously the old name for Hawkesbury, also the name of one of the pre-enclosure open fields of Foleshill and the name of an eighteenth century coalmine created in that open field.

Radford Fields c1910 (Waterman)

It is rare to get a postcard that simply records the countryside of Edwardian Coventry before the suburbs were built. It was not so spectacular in its own right that the focus of a road or a building was considered necessary to gain the interest of a purchaser. This view of Radford Fields slipped through the net as the snow covered ground was the main interest but it does make it more difficult to tie down its exact location. The stream is Radford Brook in the area north of where the Radford Hotel is found today.

Engleton Road c1922 (Ralph's Real Photos)

The first fruits of the construction by the City Council of improved sanitary services can be seen in this view of new housing, also showing a little bit of what was left of Radford Common. The war memorial is in the foreground with Engleton Road, leading to Moseley Avenue on the right. German prisoners of war from the 1914-18 conflict, who were based in nearby Villa Road, supposedly helped in its construction. The memorial has now been moved to the opposite side of the road.

Radford Road c1936 (Unknown)

This postcard showing the "Grapes Inn" will confuse today's residents of the area, as it is on the opposite side of the Radford Road to it's present position. The view is looking up the rise in the road towards the City centre, with Swillington Road being just around the bend to the left. The driver of the cart parked outside in what would now be a very dangerous spot, was possibly enjoying a pint of Bass bitter with the publican A.J. Jarrard. The railings seen on the right are still in existence, in places, above what is now Bridgeman Road.

Lydgate Road 1923 (Unknown)

This interesting group of motorcyclists, members of the Coventry Triangle Motor Club, are seen turning left from Lydgate Road on to the Radford Road. They are taking part in the Coventry Hospital Carnival event, which took place on Saturday 9th June to mark the 50th anniversary of the Hospital Saturday Movement. The event which started from the Radford Aerodrome, Middlemarch Road, raised £2,888 towards the upkeep of the hospital, which was heavily in debt and due to its success became an annual event.

Daimler Works c1909 (Harvey Barton)

Sandy Lane c1907 (Waterman)

This disused cotton mill near the Coventry canal basin became the home of Britain's first motor car factory in 1896. The mill, burnt out in 1891 had been reconditioned and was empty, just at the time when the syndicate who had bought the rights to produce the Daimler car in this country were looking for a suitable site. Luckily for Coventry it was chosen in place of Birmingham and Cheltenham, the other main locations considered. The 13 acre site was quickly developed, the original cotton mill building being converted into a three-tier machine shop. In 1908 when further expansion was not possible, the site at Radford was acquired, which luckily became the main works. In 1937 the Coventry works were vacated, being used as an Air Ministry store when in 1940 most of the works including the cotton mill were destroyed by the Luftwaffe. The British built Daimlers as early as 1897 had gained many successes in motor trials, being awarded sixteen major prizes in the first 1000 Mile Trial in 1900. In 1907 three cars were entered in one of the world's oldest and greatest road races, the Italian Targa Floria. The bottom view shows the cars which gained 13th, 20th and 26th places, in Sandy Lane about to enter the Coventry Works. The house on the corner of St Nicholas Street is The Gables with Merrick Lodge behind.

Widdrington Road c1906 (ER)

This view looking from the Sandy Lane, Ellis Road junction shows Widdrington Road curving to the left at the far end at the connection with Dorset Road. On the right, opposite Dorset Road, would have been Duryea Motor Company, this site in later years being Coventry Climax works. It would appear to be an early morning scene with milk being delivered and children on their way to school. Francis Hegan has not yet opened Ellis Road Post Office but next door to his wife's drapers shop the manager of The London Central Meat Company has had the shop scrubbed out ready for the days business. At this time a railway line ran on the spot the cameraman is standing from the Nuneaton line, before Daimler Halt, into the Daimler Works.

"Leaving Off" at the Radford Daimler. c1926 (Teesee)

These workers are seen leaving the main entrance of the Radford Daimler works in Daimler Road. This works produced only motor vehicles until the outbreak of the First World War in 1914. Later in the war a 105 H.P. engine and transmission were developed for a tractor, to work pulling large loads in difficult conditions in France. This developed into the Tank which in late 1917 at the Battle of the Somme turned the tide of the War. The French Gnome aero engine was also produced, in large numbers and as later aeroplanes were also produced, in 1915 a 'flight ground' was built at the back of the factory. When this area was later built on it became known as the Radford Aerodrome Estate.

Radford Road c1932 (Teesee)

The local children must have known that the cameraman was due, for so many of them to gather on the Radford Road, outside the Radford Social Club. The view is looking towards the city with Dugdale Road on the right, and further down Wyley Road with the shops between. The children would have gone to the Radford Council School further down on the right, the other side of Lawrence Saunders Road.

The Radford Garage c1929 (Unknown)

This advertising postcard would have been used by T.H. Hunter to gain new customers to his Radford Road Garage. The Garage was next to the Radford Congregational Chapel, near to the intersection with Villa Road. At the time the Radford Hotel was being built but it would still be some years before the Savoy Cinema was erected. Cars were still beyond the reach of the working man, petrol being as much as $1/4^{1/2}$ a gallon (7p) and lubricating oil 9d pint (4p). Today this is the Savoy Service Station.

Peel-Connor Telephone Works, Coventry.

Peel-Connor Telephone Works, c1925 (Teesee)

Aerial View of Peel-Connor Works 1926 (Aerofilms)

These workers leaving the recently constructed telephone works of Peel-Connor in Stoke were part of the Coventry "Silicon Valley" of their day. Together with British Thomson Houston, already established in Coventry since 1912, they made a significant contribution to the burgeoning electrical industry in this country. Sadly, these well dressed and often highly skilled workers who were to establish Coventry as a centre of electrical excellence, would be disappointed to see how run-down the industry was to become by the 1980's. As can be seen from the aerial photograph, the size of the factory from its very earliest phase was an impressive investment. The view points in a south easterly direction, with Brindle Avenue to the left, Telephone Road to the right and the junction of Crescent Avenue and Uxbridge Avenue at the bottom of the picture. The junction of these two roads can be seen to the left of the top picture looking towards the top of Telephone Road.

AEROFILMS SERIES   AERIAL VIEW OF PEEL-CONNER TELEPHONE WORKS, STOKE, COVENTRY   No. C 499

Binley Road, Stoke, Coventry.

Binley Road c1924 (HHT)

Tram, Binley Road c1938 (Unknown)

These two views show approximately the same location but looking in opposite directions. The first view is looking towards town near to where the Peel-Connor (GPT) Works had been built on the left, though Uxbridge Avenue has yet to be built. In the second, later picture, the tram is heading back towards town from the Uxbridge Avenue Terminus. The tram lines were not extended to this Terminus until 1930, so before this the trams turned around by the Bulls Head Inn, near Bray's Lane. On the left of the second picture can be seen the construction of houses in the Bromleigh Drive area. This development was to take over what is still shown as countryside on the right hand side of the earlier view, with Momus Boulevard flanking the road.

Binley Road c1924 (HHT)

Despite the fact that these houses had been erected before the First World War, one side of Binley Road still resembles a country lane. This photograph was taken just beyond the Bull's Head tram terminus, towards Binley. Stoke Rectory is in the distance on the left, by Church Lane. Though the north side of the road has been developed, the south side is fenced off where the Coventry & North Warwickshire sport ground remains today, though the frontage by the road has now been developed for housing and a petrol station. This side of the road was paved soon after the time of this picture as Biggin Hall Crescent and Crescent Avenue were built to fill the gap to the Peel-Connor Works beyond.

Siddeley Avenue c1931 (Teesee)

At last a Coventry avenue that actually has trees! Although they have not yet been planted at the time this photograph was taken, it is clear by the scene today that they were soon afterwards. The building work on Siddeley Avenue is not quite finished as can be seen by the gables being completed on the houses to the left with the builders' lorry in the street. The houses on the left are, however, shown occupied with curtains in the windows and the chain link fencing that was not to survive the salvaging forays of the Second World War. The residents today suffer from the lack of foresight that created such a narrow road, yet this picture shows that traffic was not an issue then.

Employees Leaving Humber Works c1908 (W.Y.)

Humber Road c1910 (Unknown)

This photograph was taken soon after the opening of the new Humber works in Humber Road, Stoke on June 30th 1908. It shows the workers leaving the factory with the houses of Stoke Green clearly visible at the top left. This was the latest of a number of ill fated car factories that Humber had occupied since they started making cars in Coventry in 1898. Their previous factories seemed to be rather more susceptible to fire than other manufacturers of the time. However the 1908 factory, built on a green-field site was sufficiently big for them to close down their Nottingham operations. More importantly it has survived until the present day as part of the Peugeot-Talbot company, though sadly some of the original brick office buildings that acted as the presentable facade to the manufacturing area have recently been demolished. These buildings can be seen in the second picture looking up the recently widened Folly Lane, now called Humber Road, towards Binley Road.

Walsgrave Road c1906 (E.R.)

Stoke Band of Hope, Walsgrave Road c1907 (Unknown)

These rare views of Walsgrave Road show the area of Ball Hill also known at the time as Stoke Knob, still almost rural with the trees of the countryside visible beyond. The first view shows a newly constructed terrace of buildings. Similar ones were soon to line the Walsgrave Road as far as Stoke church. The Old Ball Hotel is one of the few survivors today from this earlier period of village scenery, but even that was rebuilt soon after this photograph was taken. The cottages raised above the road on the right are so typical of other lost roadscapes in Radford and Walsgrave, only to be seen still in Allesley. The local Band of Hope are parading only a few doors beyond the Old Ball, an uncomfortable reminder of the evils of drink to the customers of that pub! They are in fact outside their local Congregational church, to the left, the sign behind them states that a new church was to be built on that spot. The church eventually built turned out to be no more than a simple corrugated iron building still in use at present as a bed shop. The more substantial church shown had been standing in one form or another since 1836, but its days were numbered with the construction of Marlborough Road on the site of the half demolished cottage just beyond.

Clay Lane c1912 (Waterman)

At this time the city's recent march into the countryside had left behind some evidence of the land's former function, but the field boundary in the foreground will not survive the end of the Great War. The old bus was one of a number in local service that was commandeered to take troops to the French front. Apart from small development where the fence is, the rest of the view is similar today. The wall on the left just beyond the Villiers Street junction hides the grounds of a cottage, the home of Joshua Perkins, owner of Britannia Mill in Paynes Lane. It now surrounds a social club car park.

Walsgrave Road c1911 (Waterman)

A few years later than the pictures on the previous page the growth of Coventry has spread further along the Walsgrave Road as far as Brays Lane and Clay Lane. In the distance can be seen the point where the new houses end and the road narrows back to the country lane as it was from Gosford Green, less than a generation earlier. At the entrance to St Michaels Road on the immediate right is Vincent Wyles butchers shop now the PDSA.

Stoney Stanton Road c1907 (E.R.)

The Alma Inn with its strange barrel-shaped dormer windows survived at the junction of Howard Street and Stoney Stanton Road until 1980. Yet as the most memorable building in the view it nevertheless fails to dominate the road in the presence of the taller buildings that became more frequent in this lower part of the road. A drapers faces the pub on the opposite side of Howard Street, whilst on the other side of Stoney Stanton Road, amongst the other shops is the premises of C. Wilkins & Co, Peer-Dragoon Cycle Manufacturers. The start of Swanswell Street can be seen to the bottom right. In the distance on the left may be made out the spire of the Wesleyan Chapel.

The Rose and Woodbine c1910 (Unknown)

This rare survivor from the golden age of pub architecture can still be found in remarkably original condition very similar to when it was built in 1898. FJ Hibbel the landlord and his wife stand proudly on the step. If they could return today they may wonder where their ironwork has gone, (to their left and above the entrance). They may also wonder how the outside is lit as their wonderful gas lamps have also disappeared along with the flagpole, but otherwise, externally at least they would feel at home. The Binley Oak, featured elsewhere in this book could earn from this example.

Stoney Stanton Road c1907 (Unknown)

This view by an anonymous photographer continues the sequence of Stoney Stanton Road begun in the previous book. Looking to town it shows the tower of the Wesleyan chapel seen on the previous page. The chapel still stands, apparently unused and in rather a derelict condition. The age of the houses is given away by a tablet on one inscribed 1882. The mixture of housing with shops is not much different from today though the shops tend to be predominant now. Being on the tram route played an important part in the early development of this area between the town and Bell Green. Speciality shops and businesses did not have to rely simply on local custom. Most of the shops shown in the first picture are nothing special, being a newsagent and tobacconist and two butchers, but the distinctive sign of a pawnbrokers can also be seen in the middle shop. This was one of sixteen in the city at the time – another can be seen in the picture of Station Street East.

Stanton Street c1906 (E.R.)

To the west of Stoney Stanton Road, about a hundred yards beyond the church shown in the previous picture, was the location of Stanton Street. It has disappeared in one of the comparatively recent housing redevelopment schemes in this area. W. Sargeant Steam Bakery on the right was in fact 555 Stoney Stanton Road. The most interesting buildings are those making up the tall nineteenth century terrace just beyond the shop. They were once the home of watch manufacturers or ribbon weavers, though by then they were simply used as dwelling places. Further down the road the road to the left were a number of active watch manufacturers. Note the cobbled pavements that were common in the earliest suburbs of the city.

Tram, Priestley's Bridge 1919 (Winterbourne)

Priesley's Bridge takes the Stoney Stanton Road over the Coventry Canal, just by Ordnance Road, yet it was better known for many years as the location of the main Tram Depot to the south of the canal, with a small entrance on the east side of the road. Behind the houses facing the road it widened out to cover quite a large area with one particularly large tram shed. One of the doors to this shed can just be seen on the left of this picture. It was quite common in this period to decorate trams for special occasions and this tram from the 1920's is trying to raise money for Coventry's War Memorial that was eventually unveiled by Field-Marshal Earl Haig in 1927. This area is now the car park for an impressive new mosque.

Red Lane c1906 (E.R.)

It is so unusual now to see older houses with "top shops" in Coventry yet there were quite a number about at the turn of the century. They were an invaluable part of Coventry's industrial heritage as well as looking good, as these weavers houses on the right bear witness. Sadly these particular houses disappeared (before the First World War) along with their trade (earlier still) which makes the few remaining even more precious to preserve. Yet many of those that have survived have been so modernised that they convey little of their original function.

Courthouse Green c1907 (J.P.)

Though officially Courthouse Green, this scene on Bell Green Road was only a short distance south of Bell Green. The Weavers Arms still occupies the same position on the west side of the road, but has been replaced by a modern building. The cottages on either side of the pub are a good indication of how the pub got its name. However, the weaving industry was already virtually dead in this area and the cottages like the pub have been demolished, leaving us with just the scattered remnants of this early mixed industrial and agricultural community.

The Vicarage, Old Church Road c1907 (E.R.)

Nothing could be more removed from the present image of Bell Green than this rural picture of comfortable country living. The vicarage went with St Laurence's which was the original parish church of Foleshill and remained in use until the 1960's. A new vicarage was built in its grounds and the old one, presently undergoing renovation, has found a new use as a nursing home. Sadly, though, with its original setting and outbuildings gone it is now a shadow of its former self. Both church and vicarage are to be found in close proximity half way along Church Road, the vicarage near the road and the church set further back.

Post Office, Hall Green Road c1908 (Unknown)

A curious extension to this country cottage houses the village post office as well as general stores. It was photographed before 1910 but there is a recruiting poster by the window, more normally associated with the outbreak of the First World War. The postmistress, Mrs Ann Franklin can be seen by the gate. The post office was near the junction of Bell Green Road with Hall Green Road just by where the Rose and Crown can be seen today.

Henley Road c1907 (E.R.)

JH Flavell, baker, grocer and beer retailer occupies the rather grandly named Bell Green House to the left of this view with a curtain draped over the outside of the shop window. The shop stands opposite the junction of Bell Green Road with Henley Road, with the camera facing towards the open countryside of Henley Green. The only reference point for this view today is the row of terraced cottages furthest down on the left, that can still be found just north of Roseberry Avenue.

Armstrong Whitworth "Whitley" c1937 (Valentine's)

This unusual view shows an early production Whitley with Tiger IX engines flying over what would have been, twenty years before, the Styvechall estate of the Gregory family. In the 1920's the War Memorial Park seen in the top centre of the picture was laid out following the purchase of the land by the Coventry Corporation. In the foreground Warwick Road can be seen passing over the Railway line together with the footbridge over the Goods Yard from Grosvernor Road to Spencer Park. On the other side of Spencer Road the tennis courts and bowling greens can be seen. On the left, Asthill Grove, Humphrey Burton Road and The Hiron have been laid out, but very few houses appear to have yet been built.

Styvechall Gate c1906 (Slapoffski)

This gate which separated Earlsdon from the estate of the Gregory family was situated at the top of what was to be Earlsdon Avenue South, where it joined Styvechall Common. Behind the cameraman would have been a very narrow Kenilworth Road with open countryside beyond which would eventually become the Memorial Park. To the right can be seen the lodge to Broadwater House. The narrow path to the right which runs to the Kenilworth Road, passes in front of a cottage called The Chestnuts. Another view of this cottage can be seen on page 83 of Volume 1. Today 'The Firs' is beyond the gate to the right.

Leamington Road c1928 (Unknown)

This postcard shows the road to Leamington at the point where today Styvechall Croft meets the Leamington Road. The signpost indicates 1½ miles to Canley, the lane meeting up with Coat of Arms Bridge Road further to the left. Coventry (Broadgate) is indicated 1¼ miles to the right with Stoneleigh and Leamington 2½ and 7½ miles respectively further along the Leamington Road. Armorial Road would soon be built between Styvechall Manor House seen to the left and the Kenilworth Railway line embankment seen in the background. The Manor House has since been demolished.

Welsh Bill Protest, 1913 (Waterman)

It is interesting to see the issues that moved the Coventrian of eighty years ago; certainly matters of church and state concerned these marchers – all 2,000 of them. They were protesting about the separation of the Church of Wales from being an official part of the state. Not very important in reality but of great significance in principle. The march, made up of the congregations of many parish churches in Coventry, converged on Styvechall Hall and met in the grounds by the permission of the owner the Hon. Alexander Gregory. The family had lived there for many generations and provided the land from which Memorial Park was created. The family and the Hall are long since gone. It stood a little south of St James's Church, before the Leamington Road cut through its grounds to join up with the newly constructed Stonebridge Highway.

Leamington Road c1938 (Richards)

This view shows the uncompleted end of the Leamington Road, which with the Stonebridge Highway behind the cameraman would not be fully completed until after the War ended. The cyclists are travelling towards the City Centre, with the Baginton Road crossing just beyond the group of trees where a small island seems to have been constructed. To the right the other side of the Baginton Road is where Styvechall Hall stood before this area was developed. The first house on the left is No. 136.

Styvechall Common from Green Lane c1930 (Teesee)

Although this bungalow appears to be isolated, No2 Green Lane originally known as Bide-a-Wee still exists, being on the corner of Green Lane and Woodside Avenue North. At the time it can be seen that Coat of Arms Bridge Road, which passes across the view, beyond the telegraph pole, is still quite narrow. The footpath seen in the distance took pedestrians across Styvechall Common from Green Lane to the Kenilworth Road.

Green Lane c1931 (Teesee)

Kenpas Swimming Pool c1933 (Unknown)

Before the Kenpas Highway was built Green Lane was an important route from the Kenilworth to Leamington Roads, the road being cut in two when the Highway was opened. The top view is looking towards where the Highway will shortly cross in the distance, with Gregory Avenue on the left just past the tree and the car. All of the trees in the picture have now gone, but on the right one still remains near the entrance into Oak Tree Avenue. The lower picture will bring back happy memories to many people on the south west-side of the city in a similar way that Gosford Pool does for those on the east. The entrance into Kenpas Swimming Pool was off Green Lane on the other side of Kenpas Highway to the above picture. A small close of bungalows known as Poolside Gardens, have been built on the site. A certain amount of artistic licence has been used in this advertising postcard as none of the houses in Bathway Road or the Kenpas Highway are shown.

Moat Avenue c1931 (Teesee)

Wainbody Avenue c1931 (Teesee)

Both of these recently constructed avenues show houses, that have that uniformity and freshness. Although some drop kerbs are visible and some double gateways are to be seen, at that time very few householders would have even owned a car let alone a garage. Most of the gates have now gone, the fronts being open with cars parked in front of the houses. However, the large telegraph poles have also now gone and the trees planted soon after these pictures were taken are now fully mature. The top view is taken looking towards Kenpas Highway with Medland Avenue to the right. In the bottom view it would seem that during the War some houses on the right were destroyed in the bombing. Today two pairs of semi-detached houses Nos. 72-78 are more modern than the remainder, making it appear that two pairs were demolished. The view is looking away from the Kenpas Highway.

Kenpas Highway c1932 (Unknown)

Originally Kenpas Road, when this section of the Coventry By-pass was constructed in the early 1930's it became Kenpas Highway. This view taken from the corner of Wainbody Avenue shows the row of shops with the corner of Woodside Avenue just being out of the picture in the distance. In the foreground is Beaumonts Kenpas Supply Stores followed by the confectioner La Maison Superieure, W.A. Bales Chemist, Archie Barnacle Butcher, J.A. Fanshawe Fruiterer then J.H. Fuller Ironmonger in that order. At the far end was L.R. Hodson Newsagents and Green Lane Post Office.

Woodside Avenue c1931 (Teesee)

This postcard like the two opposite were part of a set issued soon after the Green Lane Post Office opened. The post office is seen on the end of the row of shops above, being run at that time by Mrs. I.M. Harris. The view is looking towards the Kenpas Highway, just around the bend to the left being the Green Lane Methodist Church. Today the view is very similar but mature trees now adorn the footpaths. Just behind the cameraman to his left where Regency Drive is today was Spinney Path leading to the Kenilworth Road.

Walsgrave Church c1935 (Unknown)

Before the hospital, before the traffic lights, before the dual carriageway Walsgrave village is in the period of transition during the inter-war years from the quaint village depicted in the first book to the busy thoroughfare that exists today. The road has already been widened in this picture from the situation at the beginning of the century to cope with the increasing traffic that the booming Coventry was attracting. The need for a 30mph limit is already evident. The Red Lion, just out of the picture to the right, has a notice up for its car park, a clear 'sign' of the times! The church of St Mary the Virgin and the buildings just beyond it flanking Hall Lane remain largely unaltered, the gravestones in the churchyard were landscaped away in the mid 1950's.

Sowe Common c1920 (Unknown)

The open countryside beckons and the pony and trap could easily be on route to Barnacle or Hawkesbury. Not today, however, with the M6 cutting off this end of Woodway Lane, turning it into a cul de sac. The Jolly Colliers just survived beyond the last house on the right and the houses on the left are relatively unaltered. But the wide verge that represents all that is left of the common has been cut through by a number of driveways and Ringwood Highway has been built through the land in the immediate foreground.

Old Bridge and Mill, Whitley, Coventry.

Old Bridge and Mill c1924 (HHT)

Mr. B.C. Hucks c1914 (Waterman)

Unless you are a resident of the Abbey Road area today, this view would be unknown to you. Now it has ceased to be a through road, ending just out of the picture to the right, at the rear of the Racquet Centre. However, historically, Abbey Road has always played a very important part. Before Thomas Telford built the present London Road, Abbey Road was the main coaching road from London to Holyhead. The bridge in the above picture, which still exists carried the road over the river Sherbourne. The mill seen to the left was demolished in the 1950's although it had been out of use since the end of the last century. On the other side of the bridge, up the hill, on the right was the entrance into Whitley Abbey where in April 1914, B.C. Hucks seen in the lower picture thrilled a large crowd with his upside down flying and looping the loop. He is shown in his Blèriot with 60hp Gnome Engine. Not long after his visit, with the use of German prisoners of war, Whitley Abbey Aerodrome was built, to be used by the RFC, later to become the RAF. It was purchased in 1920, for £5,000, by the Sir W.G. Armstrong Aircraft Company, many of the aircraft designed by this company being built and flown from this aerodrome. The last aircraft which took off being two prototype Whitley Bombers in 1936. Whitley was then used throughout the war for aircraft sub-assembly, the aircraft including the Lancaster Bomber being finished off at Baginton. Whitley plant was later acquired by Chrysler and is now Jaguar Engineering Centre.

Mr. B.C. Hucks at Coventry .1.

Baginton Lane c1930 (Unknown)

The Island, London Road c1957 (Landscape)

The boarded up remnants of these houses have only recently been demolished. They were to be found beside the petrol station on the west side of the A45 approaching the Willenhall roundabout. This was the original road to Baginton, a continuation of Brandon Lane, before the A45 was made into a dual carriageway. It was originally known as Rowley Lane, but when Coventry Airport was built a new road was built to Baginton, Rowley Road, that skirted the airport to the north. The second picture also testifies to the influence of the car on the landscape. When these houses were built, at the same time as those on the first picture, there was only one road at this spot, the London Road. By the Second World War the Coventry By-pass had joined it from the west. Before long it was necessary to build this roundabout to cope with the increasing traffic. Then by the late 1980's the Eastern By-pass was built to join up with it and eight of these houses were demolished and the roundabout increased in size. In the centre of this picture can be seen the pillbox built in wartime to protect this imporant route to Coventry and Birmingham.

The Island, London Road, Willenhall.

The Shops, Ansty Road c1957 (Landscape)

Where shops are concerned every picture is soon made historic as small businesses quickly rise and fall. Of Nicks greengrocers, H. Whitehead high class butchers, Robinsons Chemists, and W. Mitchell newsagent none remain with their original owners. The rest of the scene has changed in more subtle ways; the road is now cluttered with markings; there is far more street furniture than one small bus stop sign, a telephone box and a telegraph pole. Today, the trees are grown up making the view more pleasant but the traffic creates more of a visual and aural ugliness.

Kelvin Avenue c1937 (Teesee)

To the east of Sewall Highway, near its junction with Ansty Road, Kelvin Avenue had only recently been built. In fact it was not yet complete. The trees for a start which would justify its name seem to have been missed, in fact there does not even seem room for them. The pre-war railings are still there as are one lamp post on each side of the road. The end of the street and Olive Avenue beyond are still countryside – where trees can be seen!

Browning Road, Coventry.

Browning Road c 1935 (Teesee)

Hermitage Road c 1935 (Teesee)

Bright and fresh as all new estates look, there is a certain attractiveness in the clean uniformity of the architects' original plans, heightened by the use of black and white photography. Today the addition of cars, different styles of decoration and various other more substantial alterations make this more of a messy scene, especially in winter. But the compensation comes in the spring when the gardens that have been carefully tended in some cases for more than half a century bring a different brightness to the scene. The view of Browning Road is looking up from its junction with Longfellow Road. That of Hermitage Road is looking east from the crossing with Mellodew Road. It is interesting to note that in the latter picture the garden walls on the right of the road are brick but on the left and early version of reconstituted stone has been used. As the original walls only survive in patches in might be assumed that such stone always has its enemies!

Hermitage Road, Wyken.

COOMBE ABBEY

It may seem to be stretching a point to include a place seven miles from the city centre in a book on Coventry, but Coombe Abbey has a special place in the heart of many Coventrians and its future fate certainly falls into the terms of reference of this book. The future of Coombe as a public facility is a cause for great debate now that the City Council has gone into partnership with private enterprise to develop the house as a hotel, and to put aside some of the grounds as a golf course. Much depends on the treatment of the house as anything which cheapens its appearance would affect the character of the very thing that characterises the park. Yet the house is desperately in need of renovation and the public never has had easy access to the building itself. But the gardens have always been open and even if not as immaculate as shown in these pictures, they were not substantially different nor were there any no-go areas. If this was lost in the development then that would be a cause for concern.

The East Front, c1910 (Bedford Real Photo Series)

Built as a monastery in 1150 very little now survives from Coombe Abbey's days as a religious institution, but this view shows, at its lowest level, the original cloisters that still exist today. However, most of the east wing above it was only constructed in the last century by William Eden Nesfield a famous Victorian architect. This wing had a lifespan of just sixty years when it was pulled down in the 1920's. It is the modern plans for the reconstruction of this wing that have attracted some of the criticisms of the council's redevelopment plans. An extension to the building to provide more hotel rooms is important for the financial viability of the project, so it would seem an imaginative approach to use the original designs of a much praised architect to bring back to life part of Coombe's past. Doubts have been expressed, however, that the quality of the materials and the faithfullness to the original will produce an honest rendering. For the moment we can only wait and see.

The South Front, c 1910 (Bedford Real Photo Series)

The West Front, c 1910 (Bedford Real Photo Series)

The view of the south front shows even more clearly the contrast between the earlier parts of the house and the Victorian addition on the right. Whatever the architectural merit of the Nesfield addition in itself, it is a matter of opinion as to its harmonious relationship to the rest of the building. When these pictures were taken the house was still in the hands of the Craven family who had owned it for the previous three hundred years. In 1921 they sold it to John Gray, a builder grown rich on developing areas of Coventry; the original Courtaulds factory was one of his projects. It was he who demolished part of the house to make it more habitable, although even in those days there was money in bits of old houses! Gray died in the early 1960's and Coventry made one of its better buys of the Abbey and 150 acres for £36,000. The most unchanged face of Coombe, to those who knew it in the early years of the century is the West Front. The second picture shows the classical lines of William Winde's work of the late seventeenth century. But at that time there would have been no moat there. Moats are normally associated with antiquity but the one at Coombe was part of the Victorian developments.

The Cottage and Entrance to Stables c1910 (Bedford Real Photo Series)

Coombe Pool, 1916 (Sylvester)

Though in substance these buildings remain the same, the details of hedges and garden around the stables show this to be a domestic scene rather than its present stripped down functional appearance. In a prominent position is one of the family dogs, held in high esteem by the Cravens as the nearby pets' cemetery demonstrates. The second picture illustrates another aspect of the Cravens' lifestyle, proving that Abbey estate was not isolated from the community. Despite the sleet and snow on a cold March Saturday in 1916, a large number of anglers and spectators had turned out to take part in a series of angling contests at Coombe Pool, a lake even larger then than now. The conditions were not good for fishing so only two fish, (type unknown), a total of 9lb 9ozs won the main prize. A number of female anglers also took part, but no one of either gender gained enough fish to be awarded a special cup provided by the Earl of Craven, with whose permission the contest took place. However, most importantly, the coffers of the local Soldiers and Sailors fund was swollen by the fees, an important matter at that time in the First World War.

INDEX TO VOLUMES 1 AND 2

A short index such as this has inevitably to be rather selective. Particular attention has been given to any streets, factories, public houses and cinemas shown, as well as any captioned buildings.

N.B. Page numbers for Volume 1 are given in normal print, those for Volume 2 are given in bold.